THE SPIR

AUSTIN'S MOST HAUNTED PATH

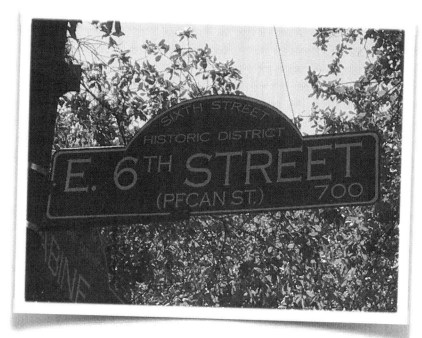

DFTB w

BY
DR. JOHN "MADMAN" MAVERICK

Cover Photo by author,
taken on a full moon lit Austin Ghost Tour

Copyright © 2017 John Maverick Magic, LLC
All rights reserved
ISBN-13: 978-1976532559

FORWARD

Welcome to my home away from home, the dirty street that Austin loves to hate, East 6th Street. I have walked this street for over two decades, collecting the legends and stories that have made this row of 19th-century buildings into the infamous party district it is today. On the surface it seems like a collection of dive bars and nightclubs but we're going to go deeper into the history, lives, and deaths of the people who lived and worked here over century ago. In the title of this book I assert that 6th Street is "Austin's Most Haunted Path." I truly believe that nowhere else in the city of Austin can you find four consecutive blocks with more stories of hauntings than on East 6th. Of course the scale is tipped with the inclusion of the Driskill Hotel, one of the most haunted hotels in the United States. Let's take a stroll down Austin's most haunted path.

THANKS

Jeanine Plumer, for giving a 20-year-old kid a chance to become a ghost tour guide oh so many years ago.

Monica Ballard, for inspiring me to finally write this book.

~~Chaz Howell~~, without you I would never have known there was such a thing as a "ghost tour."

All the bartenders, doormen, and waitstaff that I have bugged incessantly for years trying to get all the details of your supernatural encounters.

Every single person who has ever taken a tour from Austin Ghost Tours. Thank you for allowing us to live our dreams.

Finally, Mom. Without you, none of this would be possible. After all, you did introduce me to Jeanine.

Table Of Contents

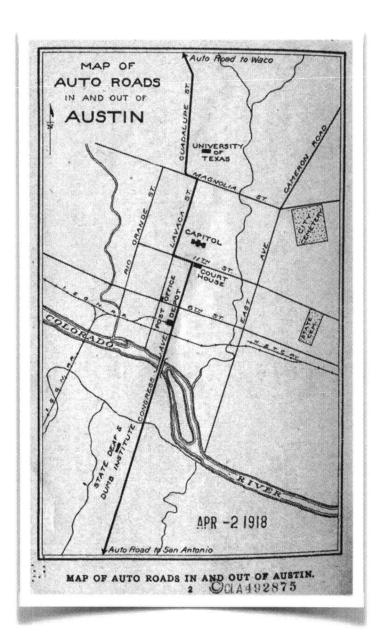

1918 map showing 6th Street as a main thoroughfare
Photo from the authors collection

A Bit of History

Ahh, 6th Street. If you live in Austin, Texas, that name can conjure images of late nights, loud music, and drinking. Mainly drinking. Most locals try to avoid it but my mother likes to make the joke that I have been going down there ever since I realized that I could ride my bike down there, and that's true. In 2000, I began giving tours of Austin with Austin Ghost Tours. I loved showing off my hometown, but I had heard so many ghost stories about 6th Street, I put together a pub crawl going up and down "Dirty 6th." The tour premiered in October of 2003 and it has always been one of my favorite tours to give. I have had my shares of adventures on 6th, some of which I am sure I can't remember, but it has a long history prior to me.

Austin was drawn out and mapped by Edwin Waller and he designed 6th street, or as he called it, Pecan Street, to be the main east to west thoroughfare. The Bastrop Highway which linked Austin to already established towns in East Texas was charted in 1839 and came into Austin along Pecan Street. It was the only street flat enough to comfortably take a wagon across town. The stagecoach

The Spirits of 6th Street: Austin's Most Haunted Path

followed this route when it arrived in Austin in 1840, and the Bullock Hotel, built in 1839 by Richard Bullock at the northwest corner of Pecan and Congress, was the stage stop. That intersection became the unofficial town square.

Not only was Pecan mostly devoid of hills but the street was far enough from the river to escape the flooding of the Colorado River which happened every few years. Austin soon became the fastest growing city in Texas and Pecan grew with it. Log and frame houses, wagon yards, boarding houses, livery stables, and saloons were built to meet the needs of travelers and the needs of a growing city.

1871 brought the train to Austin and the depot was only a few blocks off 6th. Many major businesses bought and built on Pecan to take advantage of the busy street and proximity to the train. The beautiful limestone Victorian commercial structures that line 6th Street and house bars and live music venues today were built at this time. Pecan Street and Congress Avenue were fitted with wooden boardwalks so the pedestrians didn't have to walk through the mud and muck.

The Spirits of 6th Street: Austin's Most Haunted Path

In 1886, the Driskill Hotel opened at the corner of Brazos and Pecan/6th Streets. It was publicized as "the finest hotel south of St. Louis", and it truly was. Jesse Driskill spent his entire fortune on the hotel. Today, the Driskill is also known as "the most haunted hotel in the U.S." It will have a brief mention in this book but to get the full story, see "True Haunted Tales of the Driskill Hotel: Volume 1" by Monica L. Ballard. She is a fellow tour guide for the Austin Ghost Tours and the one who inspired me to write this book.

6th Street developed a diverse culture during this period of development, but it became very pronounced in the 1890s and early 1900s. Many African American owned businesses opened, including an African American physician and even a funeral parlor. This diversity continued, grew and became one of 6th Street's most striking characteristics. Lebanese businesses also began to appear on 6th Street in the 1890s. One of the first Lebanese immigrants to Austin, Cater Joseph, opened a confectionery on Congress in the 1880s. The Joseph family still maintains a business on East 6th Street, as do several other Lebanese and Syrian families who founded businesses there in the

The Spirits of 6th Street: Austin's Most Haunted Path

early 20th century. By 1940, businesses on 6th Street were owned by Blacks, Jewish, German, Chinese, and Mexican Americans, as well.

In the 1970's dance halls and bars started to open on 6th Street. These mainly catered to the African American community but by the 1980's, everyone knew that 6th street was the place to drink and party. Today, "Dirty 6th" (as it is not-so-lovingly known) is home to over 30 bars, night clubs, and live music venues. Every weekend it becomes the biggest party in Texas with an average of 30,000 people crowding a 4 block area between Brazos and Red River Streets.

THE WILLIS BROTHERS

As with every city, Austin in 1877 had a good part of town and a bad part of town. The bad part of town was where the outlaws lived. The part of town where if you were a law man you didn't go there without three or four of your law man buddies. The part of town where if you were driving a stagecoach you had the choice of taking the long way around or riding like hell straight through. Today that area of town is known as Westlake.

Austin natives always get a giggle out of that. Today, Westlake is an affluent area of Austin. Large homes of respected people litter the limestone landscape. But why was this such a bad part of town in the old days? The answer is fairly simple: it was hard to traverse with hills and rocky crags, and the only thing you can grow in that solid stone is cedar and mosquitoes. For outlaws, it was a good place to hide out and poor folks were able to live there without paying a rich man. In that area lived a band of brothers known as the Willis Brothers, or more precisely, the Redheaded Willis Brothers. That "flaming" red hair is how they were most commonly described to the city marshal. Random fun fact: red hair was considered a sign of inbreeding back in those days… We know better now.

On, quite literally, the other side of town was a more well-to-do area. Today it is known as Hyde Park, but back in the 1870s it was full of rural farms and larger plantations. In the eastern outskirts of the area, the Texas State Fair was held from 1875 until it was moved to Dallas in 1884. A portion of the State Fair's horse racing track is still reflected in the curved segment of 39th Street between Avenue F and Duval Street. In this area you could find the home of Mr. Williams, a respectable man with plenty of money.

In those days, most people who had money didn't trust banks. People were skittish after the first financial collapse of 1873, not to mention the banks were common targets for outlaws. Most folks kept their money buried in a tin chest somewhere on their property. Mr. Williams had a better idea. He put his money in a burlap sack and then locked the sack in a cedar chest by the foot of his bed. His attitude was, "I've got guns, I can protect my family and my money." His flaw was telling everyone his plan. I can just picture him one night at a saloon on old Pecan Street touting his masterful security system and a Willis Brother overhearing the plan.

One morning in 1877, three of the Willis brothers road up to the Williams estate with 20 hired Native Americans. They performed a traditional Indian raid, arrows flying and bullets firing. As they rode up to the main house, they found the three Williams children playing outside. They didn't want to leave any witnesses or any evidence so they killed the children. One of the Willis brothers got off his horse and went in the house. From the house, a scream was heard. It was Mrs. Williams, who was then murdered and the Willis brother was seen to leave the house with a bag. Mr. Williams was not in the house. Guessing that he might be in the barn bridling a horse to try to escape, another Willis brother rode over. No sound was overheard from the barn but Mr. Williams was there and he was murdered. The Willis brothers than set fire to all the buildings on the property, leaving no witnesses and no evidence.

The Spirits of 6th Street: Austin's Most Haunted Path

You maybe asking yourself, "If there were no witnesses or evidence, how do you know the story?" Well, I left out one small detail. A detail about the size of a seven-year-old girl. I told you that the Williams had three children when they really had four. Their youngest, a seven-year-old girl whose name has been lost to time (we simply know her as the surviving Williams child) was able to hide and escape the Willis brothers. When the neighbors saw smoke rising from the fires, they quickly rushed to help the family put out the flames only to find this young girl crying over the body of her dead brother.

They asked her, "What happened?"

She said, "Indians attacked… Oh, yeah, and there were three redheaded man."

That was all the Austin City Marshall needed to round up the Willis brothers. The young girl identified John, Jay, and Jim Willis and they stood trial for the crime. The judge declared that, "Never in Texas, nor the United States, have three men been put to death on the word of a child. And so not in Austin." The Willis Brothers were free to go. Before the men could celebrate, the judge added, "But they are Willis brothers so they've probably done something bad. A night in jail for the three of them." I personally believe that the judge did this for his own safety.

The citizens of Austin were not pleased with his ruling. That night, roughly 60 men gathered in our town Square, 6th and Congress, with the intent to do something about the judges ruling. If the Willis Brothers had escaped back into the forests of cedar on the western side of town, those men just might have marched to the judge's house that night. Instead they marched up Congress Avenue to the courthouse where the Willis brothers were being held. The men pounded on the jailhouse door. Two armed guards answered and the mob shouted, "Hand over the Willis brothers or we'll hurt you bad!" And the armed guard said, "… Sure come on in." They didn't like the Willis brothers either. The Willis brothers were abducted.

Journal entries from the men who committed this deed proudly boast about how tightly they tied the ropes around the Willis's wrists. They were kicked out of the front door of the jail house, marched down Congress

The Spirits of 6th Street: Austin's Most Haunted Path

Avenue, and beaten as they walked to the eastern side of 6th street, to Waller Creek. That area of town was known as the "Town Commons" and was owned by a man named John O'Connor. The commons was filled with large oak trees growing on rocky soil. This unique environment made the trees grow slowly, with large branches hanging low, only slightly above the head of a man. These were Austin's hanging trees.

A rope was thrown over a low hanging branch and a Willis brother was tied to the rope. This was not a traditional Hangman's noose but a square knot: the condemned man was already choking before a few large men picked up the other end of the rope and simply pulled. One at a time, the Willis brothers were raised in to the trees, just high enough to watch them kick. This is a slow death, an asphyxiation or choking death. It can take up to eight minutes for a man to die this way... or so I've been told.

They say that two of the Willis brothers went without a word while the third screamed the entire way. We have this account in many journal entries. Although only 60 men began this lynching, somewhere between 200 and 500 people were at the final murder of the Willis brothers. And yes, while some people might refer to this as justice, it was technically murder. The Willis brothers had been acquitted and innocent in the eyes of the law. This was an act performed by good, upstanding Austinites. No one was ever charged for the murder of the Willis brothers, we can only assume that most of the law men in Austin were on scene lending a hand.

This was far from an isolated incident. The hanging trees had seen use for years before and it continued for years afterwards. There isn't a particular ghost in the hanging trees but the area is one of the darkest in downtown Austin. I don't mean this metaphorically but truly physically. I dare you to visit the area at night. Only a few blocks away are live music venues of the "Live Music Capital of the World", but along Waller Creek is a dangerous area that should be avoided by locals and tourists alike. My personal belief is that all the negativity, up to 100 souls lost in those trees through the years, has scarred the land to make it what it is today. It is the one area of downtown that I don't walk alone and caution everyone against. Do us all a favor and don't go there.

CASINO EL CAMINO

517 E 6th Street, Casino El Camino Photo by author

If you are ever looking for me on a Friday or Saturday night after a ghost tour, a safe bet would be 517 E. 6th Street, better known as Casino El Camino. This dive bar is known for its award winning burgers, cheesy movies, and killer jukebox. But in an upstairs back room, lovingly called "The Diablo Room," strange things occur that most patrons never hear about.

The Spirits of 6th Street: Austin's Most Haunted Path

The first time I remember hearing about the ghost at Casino El Camino, I was only 21 years old. I had gone in one afternoon for a burger and a beer, or as I called it back then, "Breakfast." I was sitting alone at the bar, watching the Simpsons with the bartender who was the only other person besides the guy working in the kitchen. I noticed the cook going up and down the back stairs several times before he walked to the bar and slammed his fist down saying, "I'm going to need a shot if I'm going to keep working here one more minute." I inquired as to what was going on and he said, "The ghost is messing with me." Of course I asked him for his story.

He had gone upstairs to a secondary bar where supplies for the kitchen were stored. The bar upstairs was only open once or twice a year for busy nights and has subsequently been closed and torn down. He went up there, opened up a locked cabinet, took out what he could carry of what he needed, and proceeded back downstairs. He had left the cabinet open because he was going to go back for more stuff. When he went back only a few moments later, the cabinets were closed and locked. He opened the cabinets back up, but closed and locked them because if they're going to be closed and locked, he's going to be the one to do it. When he went back up for the third time a few moments later, the cabinets were unlocked and waiting for him. I bought him his shots because I had my first ghost story about Casino El Camino.

I continued to frequent Casino El Camino, as I still do today, and the stories have continued. Most of them have to do with that back room.

One waitress back then, Amanda, had the most stories. Almost every time I would walk in, she would have something new. Many of her stories were about things moving in the Diablo Room, candles being lit before she had a chance to light them or glassware being collected from around the room to one central location when no one else was around. One story stood out because it happened so frequently and not just to her. The story had to do with the double doors at the back of the room which led out to the back patio.

The doors are constructed in such a way that if you close and lock the door on the left, the one on the right cannot be opened. There were two latches at the top of the doors where a bolt needed to be pushed up to lock them. Needless to say, gravity could not accidentally lock the doors. But they would mysteriously lock, quite often as Amanda was walking up the back stairs to the Diablo Room. She would hear the bolt click as she neared the door, preventing her from getting through the doors. She would look through the windows and there was never anyone in the room that might have locked her out or that could let her in. She once reported that this happened to her three times in a single night.

One beautiful autumn evening, I was leading a Pub Crawl into Casino El Camino and a couple of ghost hunters, Sean and Erik, were tagging along. They had taken the tour several times and had brought along several "toys" to help them find ghosts. As I was standing out front giving my introduction to the bar and directions to the Diablo Room, Sean went on inside the bar. After getting my beer (it was a Pub Crawl after all) I found him in the Diablo Room with a laser thermometer pointed at those double doors. This fun little device can give you a temperature reading from the other side of the room.

Being the sarcastic, jaded, and snarky individual I am, I just had to make the snide remark of, "Find the ghost yet?" Looking at the thermometer he replied, "Not sure." He showed me the thermometer and I saw a reading of 30 degrees. He aimed the thermometer at the wall on the left side of the room and got a reading of 72. Aiming the laser back at the door, I saw a reading of 29. A quick check of the wall on the right side showed 74 degrees. One more time at the double doors gave a reading of 64, which was the temperature outside that evening.

The Diablo Room, Photo by author

The Spirits of 6th Street: Austin's Most Haunted Path

There are no air conditioner vents or cold water lines along that back wall, and Sean wasn't aiming the laser at his drink to try to trick me. I have tried every way I can think of to explain away this phenomenon, but I have been left dumbfounded. A negative temperature change has been associated with the presence of a spirit since ancient times. I guess that explanation will have to work for me.

After the Pub Crawl, Sean and Erik returned to Casino El Camino to do some more investigating. They spent several minutes in the Diablo Room trying to find an explanation to the cool temperature readings, which they were not able to duplicate. They also spent several minutes playing with the deadbolts on the back door to see if there was anyway to get them to latch accidentally. After coming up with nothing, they decided to make their way down the back stairs to the patio. As they got to the bottom of the stairs, a young couple passed them on their way up to the Diablo Room. When the couple got to the double doors, they were locked out. The couple turned around and asked Sean and Erik if they had locked the doors. At this point, the ghost hunters began snapping photo after photo of the doors. Several days later, they showed me the the photos which had some evidence of orbs or streaks of light with unknown origins, but there was one photo that struck me more than the others. In only this one photo, it looked to me as if there was a shadow looking out the window of the left side door. The shape of the face I saw looked female to me.

This inspired me to ask more direct questions of the bar staff about their experiences in the Diablo Room. I returned that evening and found Amanda hard at work. I asked her, not if she had any new experiences but what she thought of the ghost.

"I like her. She's like a playful child!" was Amanda's response.

I had to inquire further, "You think the ghost is female?"

"For sure." She continued, "In fact I have given her a name. I call her Mary."

The Spirits of 6th Street: Austin's Most Haunted Path

This sent me back to my history notes of the building. The structure was originally built in the 1872 by a German family and operated as a dry goods store. The second floor was rented out as a boarding house. At that point, what is now the Diablo Room was a back porch. In 1906, it was sold to a Lebanese family whose patriarch was named Selim Fayad. The Fayad's enclosed the upstairs porch to make room for their growing family, including a few children that were born in the residence. In 1916 a young daughter, only one year old, passed away in the upstairs home of the Fayad's. The child's name was Mary.

The evidence had lead me to a name and I was so excited to announce her name on my next tour. As I finished the story and told my guests what I had found, I had chills down my spine. When I said her name for the first time in the Diablo Room, the crowd was visibly moved and a few people noted that it made the hairs stand up on the back of their necks. I was sure that I had found who was haunting Casino El Camino, but the real evidence came much slower.

The Spirits of 6th Street: Austin's Most Haunted Path

A few weeks later, I asked Amanda if she had any new encounters. She looked at me surprised and told me that all had been quiet. A few months pass and nothing. Almost a year went by and I was starting to think that I had scared Mary away by saying her name. I even began telling people that Casino El Camino was no longer haunted. But Mary came back. It was a full year after I said her name that she returned like nothing had happened. In fact, she was locking the back doors so much that management removed the deadbolts to put an end to her mischief.

Casino El Camino will always be one of my favorite haunts on 6th Street. I visit the bar most weekends before and after tours. I still get new stories about Mary and I will continue to raise a pint to her memory. The best part? She let's me say her name now.

222 EAST 6TH STREET

222 E 6th Street, Photo by author

At the time of this writing, 222 E. 6th Street is mainly a vacant building except for a small portion which has been opened as Recess Bar. But being vacant is what most people know this building for. Built in the 1870's, it was originally two separate buildings that have both been a myriad of different businesses through the years. In the 1970's, the buildings were combined and converted into a movie theatre called Studio 42 which showed films of an adult nature.

Over the past 20 years, most of the time it has stood empty and decaying. In my youth, the establishment was open as "The Inferno," a pop music dance club. The third floor was once opened for a short time as a stand alone bar with a Gothic theme, candle lit and spooky. You had to go up the fire escape to reach the bar and the inside was falling apart even then.

The first ghost story I heard about the building dates back to this time. There was an old upright piano in the corner of the bar, it had been there when they moved in and no one knew where it had come from. If you tried to play the piano, the only sound you would hear was your fingers hitting the ivory keys. After hours, it was a different story. Bar staff would report that as they left at night they would hear the piano start to play was if it was in an old saloon. Unfortunately, the piano has been lost to time and I never experienced this particular haunting.

The Spirits of 6th Street: Austin's Most Haunted Path

In the Spring of 2002, I was walking by and was shocked to see the place being completely gutted. I made a few inquiries and all I could get was that a "major chain" had leased the space and was remodeling it. The remodel was extensive. The 3rd floor was in such disrepair that they had to completely remove it. A colony of a few thousand bats had moved in and their guano had rotted the support beams. I snuck in a few times to ask if anything strange had been seen while they were working and I was repeatedly but politely asked to leave by a very large foreman who laughed at my "spook stories."

A few months later, and the announcement was made public, the Hard Rock Café was opening at 222 6th Street. I was excited. Finally, a place that would stay open for long enough for me to get some good ghost stories. I was there opening night and I met the manager. I introduced myself saying, "I'm Maverick. I'm with the Austin Ghost Tours and this building is haunted. Let me know if you see anything."

He smiled an ear-to-ear grin. This gentleman had been sent to Austin by the corporate office from his position at the Hard Rock Café in New Orleans. In New Orleans, they don't just like ghosts, they are competitive with their ghosts. He looked me right in the eyes and said, "Maverick, I'm going to find you that ghost." We shook hands and I left to go give my tour.

I came back that night, not expecting much, I was just excited. No ghost yet, but I knew a good story was right around the corner. A week later, nothing. Weeks turned into months without a new ghost story. We started to think that the extreme renovations had also removed the hauntings. This may seem like a joke but it has been known to happen when older buildings are changed drastically or moved. I must admit, I gave up on 222 E. 6th Street.

It became an honorable mention on the Haunted 6th Street Pub Crawl, a time killer for when people were not drinking on the tour so we were ahead of schedule. One summer night, a full year after the Hard Rock Café opened, I had one such tour. I stopped out front and began telling the group the story I have just told you. As I am talking, a young lady that worked in the Hard Rock souvenir shop stuck her head out to listen to my story. I ended my tale with, "Unfortunately, we now believe that this location is no longer haunted."

The souvenir shop girl timidly raised her hand and said, "Um…yes, it is." The entire group abruptly turned to look at her. She shrank back, "I'm not sure if I am allowed to talk about it…"

"Oh no, you totally are!" I encouraged her, "I know the manager and he wants the building to be haunted." She then cautiously told us a story about the little room just above where we were standing. The three windows on the second floor which look directly into the ladies restroom.

She had been in the restroom one day before work, using the mirror to do her makeup. As she looked into the mirror she saw the handicapped stall door, the only one facing the mirror, open very slightly. Just large enough for someone to poke their head out the door. She couldn't get the feeling out of her mind that someone or something was watching her from that stall. Exasperated, she turned around to face the stall door. After a moment, nothing happened so she returned to the mirror to continue with her makeup. She looked at the door one final time and it suddenly slammed shut. She grabbed her makeup and ran downstairs. She had never mentioned it to anyone. She was afraid that she would be fired by the big corporate Hard Rock Café for telling stories.

Armed with this new story, I came back after the tour that night. I found the manager and told him what I had heard. At the young lady's request, I kept her anonymous, she was still fearful that she might get in trouble. The manager was ecstatic! He said, "We have an employee meeting tomorrow. I will get you more stories." He was a man of his word. Most of the employees had stories, they were all just too nervous to share. They were scared of losing their jobs if they made a big deal. Most of the stories had to do with that ladies restroom.

One of my favorites came from a bartender that had been serving a bachelorette party. It was seven young ladies all celebrating together. Then, all the young ladies decided to go to the restroom as a group. As a man, this is a concept I do not understand. There are two sinks in the bathroom and as each of the young ladies finished with what they had gone there to do, they went to the sinks to wash up. The

The Spirits of 6th Street: Austin's Most Haunted Path

final young lady went to wash her hands and as she reached for the faucet knobs they both slowly turned on for her. She jumped back and asked her friends if the sinks automatically turned on. All of her friends shook their heads and questioned her as to why. She told them what had happened and as she did she mimicked reaching for the knobs. At that moment the sink slowly turned off. A few of the girls screamed at this point. She reached one more time to attempt to turn on the faucet and at that point both sinks turned on full stream and all seven young ladies ran screaming out of the bar. They elected one of the girls to go back inside to pay the tab. When the bartender asked why they had ran out, she gave him this very strange account.

The Hard Rock Café became a regular stop on the tour. One evening as I was taking a group in, a young lady on the tour laughed out loud and said, "I knew it was haunted!" before I told her the stories, I asked her if she had one. Of course, it had to do with the ladies restroom. She works downtown and had visited the Hard Rock Café for lunch with a friend a few weeks before. She had gone to the restroom and decided to use the handicapped stall, her reasoning was because it has more room than a regular stall. When she went in, the stall door was wide open. She attempted to close it but the door would not shut. It stayed firmly open as if it was tethered to the wall. She reached behind the door looking for where it might be latched, but could not find a connection. She pulled one more time on the door and it swung easily. She used the facilities as she had planned and then spent a moment playing with the door to see if she could get it to stay open again. She could not.

She then began to walk to the sink to wash her hands, but as she was walking, the venetian blinds on the windows slowly opened as she passed. To this day, I am still amazed that I had to be the one to confirm that yes, that room is haunted. For obvious reasons, I have never been in that room. I wait for the day when that section of 222 E. 6th Street is once again open and we can see what lingers.

THE HANNIG BUILDING

204 E 6th Street, Photo by author

The building at 204 E 6th Street is home to B. D. Riley's Irish Pub and was built in 1876 by J. W. Hannig, a cabinetmaker who was married to a true legend of Texas history, Susanna Dickinson. Susanna Dickinson was the only English-speaking survivor of the Alamo and J. W. Hannig was her fifth husband, who was also 15 years her junior. She liked to survive. They lived in a large home, built in 1869 in what is now Hyde Park.

The Spirits of 6th Street: Austin's Most Haunted Path

The home is now a museum dedicated to the family and other survivors of the Alamo.

Susanna Dickinson, authors collection

When this building was built, the first floor was Mr. Hannig's shop, the second floor was rented out as office space, and the third floor were rented boarding rooms. Currently the second and third floors are rented out as office space and the first floor is home to B. D. Riley's Irish Pub. It is a true Irish pub in that the decor, bar, and fixtures were brought over piece by piece from Ireland.

Besides tables, chairs, and cabinets, there was one piece of furniture that Mr. Hannig was known for making. A piece of furniture that everyone is going to need at one point in their life: coffins. These were the days prior to funeral homes and many cabinet makers were also part-time morticians. If you happened to pass away back in the days of J. W. Hannig, you would quickly be visited by a carpenter.

First, you would be placed on a board known as a "cooling board" that would be the approximate size of an average coffin. This served the purpose of getting your body in the right position to be placed in a coffin prior to rigor mortis setting in. Very rarely does anyone die in a perfect lying down position.

Next, the carpenter would take out a piece of string to get your basic measurements. Coffins were built to order and they wanted to make sure that each was a perfect fit. They called this, "being fitted for your wooden overcoat." (The Victorians tended to be a bit morbid.)

Then, once your coffin was finished, you would be put on display at J. W. Hannig's shop. These are also the days of postmortem photography. Often, your casket would be propped up, with your family gathered around and one final photo would be taken of the group. Your friends and family would bring flowers in say their final goodbyes. Not because they're pretty but because they are fragrant and you have been dead for up to 24 hours at this point.

Finally, your body would be taken to a plot in the Oakwood Cemetery and buried. If you had the money, a grave marker would be placed a few weeks later. All in all, it was a very quick turnaround. They wanted to get bodies in the ground as fast as possible. Today's preservation and refrigeration technology allows us to keep our loved ones around until it is convenient for us.

Most of the stories that I've heard about this building come from B.D. Riley's Pub and most of those stories came from a manager named Steve. Steve was first one there in the mornings to unlock and receive deliveries before other people came in to prepare for lunch. One morning he goes in and walks behind the bar. He hears footsteps walking around the far side of the bar and then hears a barstool be pulled out along the tile floor. He assumed that he had forgotten to lock the door behind him and a patron had come in off the street. When he looked across the bar he was surprised to see no one sitting there. He walked around the far side of the bar to where he had

The Spirits of 6th Street: Austin's Most Haunted Path

heard the barstool being pulled out and to his surprise a barstool had been moved, even though no one else was in the bar.

Steve knew it had been moved because he had just walked by a few moments before and everything had still been in place. He went to go double check that the door was locked and in fact it was. He just chalked it up to another unexplained experience in his haunted pub.

Upstairs an apparition of a lady wearing Victorian era clothing has been seen walking the hallways. Often she is attributed with closing doors and unexplained knocking sounds. They call her, "The House Mother" and it is believed that she is the matron of the former boarding rooms. Some people believe that it is in fact the ghost of Susanna Dickinson although we do not have any record of her being the matron. Although I do not believe it is she, I can understand why people would want the ghost of a Texas legend keeping an eye on them.

BUFFALO BILLIARDS

201 E 6th Street, Buffalo Billiards, Photo by author

There has been a structure on the southeast corner of 6th and Brazos Streets since 1841. The original wood frame structure was known as the Missouri house. It was built as a boarding house for working men who were coming to the new Austin City looking for work. In 1871 the Missouri house was torn down and replaced by two brick structures. Over the next 50 years, the one on the western side of the property was everything from a ladies clothing store to a saloon, while it's neighbor was, for the most part, a grocery store. In the early 1920s, David Gellman combined both buildings to house Gellman's Department Store.

Way back in 2002, I would go into Buffalo Billiards to inquire about ghosts. I had heard stories dating back to when the bar was called "Hang'em High Saloon," but I wasn't sure if anyone there currently had any stories. I was greeted by a manager named Sean who was not only excited to tell me his stories but took me on an hour long adventure throughout the building telling me every ghost story he had ever heard about the place.

His first story had happened to him when he was still fairly new to the establishment. He was coming into work one morning, the first one to arrive, and as he walked past the front windows he could clearly see balls out on the billiards tables. They take great pride in their billiards tables at Buffalo Billiards and every night the balls are put away and the tables dusted off. Since he had been the one to close the night before, he knew that no balls had been left on the tables. Clearly someone had been in there when they weren't supposed to be. He rushed to the front door and as he unlocked it he expected to hear the alarm going off. Not only was the alarm silent but every door was locked and there was no other evidence of anyone having been in there since he had left the previous night.

Upstairs there is a room known as the Lodge. It is the largest room in the establishment and features a large round, concrete bar in the middle of the room. One night Sean was working that bar. After closing, he was the only one upstairs. He was counting out the money in the register when to his right a barstool began to shake violently as if someone was manhandling it to try to get his attention. He didn't want to be bothered with yet another ghost so he turned his back to the barstool. In the time it would take someone to walk around to the opposite side of the bar, a barstool which was now right in front of him began to shake in the same way. He grabbed the register drawer and took it downstairs to count his money in the office.

I have also had my fair share of experiences in Buffalo Billiards. In fact I can honestly say that I have had more experiences in that building than anywhere else. My first experience happened the very first night I ever led a

The Spirits of 6th Street: Austin's Most Haunted Path

ghost tour into Buffalo Billiards. I was standing in the Lodge with my back to one of the corners of the room. The only lights on in that room that particular evening were the wall sconces. I was speaking to a group of 12 people and as a professional orator I am continually trying to make eye contact with each and every one of my guests. As my eyes traveled from left to right, I saw what appeared to be a person walking from right outside my peripheral vision to directly underneath the nearest sconce. My eyes were tracking away from this, but moments later I looked back and just as I was getting to this person, they vanished before my eyes. I tried my best to ignore it. (After all, a good storyteller doesn't get distracted.) But as it vanished, two young ladies standing very nearby jumped and stared at where it had been.

Breaking from my story I asked the young ladies if they had just seen someone stand there and then abruptly vanish. They both nodded with a mixture of fear and excitement. I was amazed that I had had an experience in this building, not only during a ghost tour, but during my first tour there. I was truly hopeful that this would not be a chance happening. It was not.

The Spirits of 6th Street: Austin's Most Haunted Path

Only one month later, I was giving a tour to a group of ladies who were all members of a book club. They had just read a book about a ghost and decided to take a ghost tour as a group. This was a special private tour and it took place in the early evening. Sean was nice enough to let us in before the bar had even opened. Once again, I was in the Lodge, but this time I was standing next to the bar. I was telling Sean's story of the vibrating barstool and I said, "The ghost in this room just seems to want to get attention." As if on cue, a stack of martini glasses at the far end of the bar was shoved over. They did not simply fall. There was glass by my boots, a full 20 feet away from where they had been stacked.

The ladies unanimously decided that it was time to make our leave. As we went downstairs, Sean was seated at the bar. I mentioned to him that some glasses had been pushed over while I was telling my story and there was broken glass everywhere. He asked, "Were the glasses stacked? He always seems to knock over stacked glasses."

The Spirits of 6th Street: Austin's Most Haunted Path

A few years later, Austin Ghost Tours was making a documentary about ghosts in Austin. We did a "ghost hunt" at Buffalo Billiards, trying to find evidence to back up our stories. We begin our search at 2 AM. I had a cameraman follow me throughout the establishment for hours. Nothing happened. There were two other groups, each with their own cameraman and we could hear them occasionally find something or have a strange reading on one of their devices. After several hours of absolutely nothing happening we heard a loud commotion from downstairs. The cameraman had a forlorn look on his face, he wanted to experience something supernatural. I told him to run downstairs and see what was going on, because nothing was happening here.

I was in a room adjacent to the Lodge, called Orbitz Lounge. There were no lights on in this room at all. The only light was what was coming in from the street lights through very dirty windows. I knew that there was a bar along the side of the room so I put my left hand on it so I wouldn't bump into anything. The barstools had all been put up onto the bar for easier cleaning the next morning. As I continued walking alongside the bar, I knew I was coming to the wall. I put my right hand out in front of me so that I wouldn't walk face first into it. When I reached the wall, I paused. I said to myself, "Nothing is going to happen to me here tonight."

I turned to retrace my steps, this time with my right hand on the bar. After walking only a few feet I bumped into something. A barstool had been taken off the bar and put in my path. I was taken aback by this. I had walked there only a moment before and the barstool had not been there. I took this is an invitation from the ghost and sat down. I reached across the bar, grabbed a glass, and poured myself a soda. I sat there until 5 AM when we called it a wrap. Although I didn't get anything on film, I felt it was the ghost's way of letting me know that I am a storyteller, not a ghost hunter.

I later found out that this is a common haunting in Orbitz Lounge. The ghost likes to put barstools in people's paths.

THE DRISKILL

E 6th & Brazos Streets, Photo by author

Full disclosure: the ghosts at the Driskill will be little more than an honorable mention in this book. This is not because it is not haunted, but because so much has already been written about the ghosts in this illustrious hotel that I feel I only have one story to add. If you want more stories about the Driskill, I recommend *True Haunted Tales of the Driskill Hotel* by Monica Ballard.

The Spirits of 6th Street: Austin's Most Haunted Path

The Driskill hotel opened on December 20, 1886. It was built by Colonel Jesse Driskill, a cattle baron from South Texas. Colonel Driskill owned Texas Longhorn cattle. Back in the pre-Civil War days, Longhorn cattle were not the cultural icons that they are today. In fact, nobody really liked them. They are skinny, they are mean, and they have really big horns. That's three reasons to not like a cow.

After the Civil War, when half the nation was starving, longhorns started to look pretty good. So Colonel Driskill and his sons took the cattle north on the Chisholm Trail and sold them off for a fortune. To give you an idea of how much money they made, visit the lobby of the Driskill Hotel. They brought all

Jesse Driskill Portrait
Driskill Hotel Lobby
Photo by author

their money to Austin, which was the fastest growing Texas city in those days, and looked for a place to invest their money. They quickly decided on building a fine hotel. They publicized the hotel as "the Finest Hotel South of St. Louis," and it truly was.

They spared no expense on their fine hotel. One problem with sparing no expense is that you can quickly run out of money. Colonel Driskill wasn't worried. He figured that anyone who was anyone was going to want to come stay in his fine hotel. Unfortunately for him, things didn't work out that way. The winter of 1886 was one of the coldest winters Austin has ever seen. There was snow on the ground on Christmas Day. That winter was following one of the longest and harshest droughts Austin has seen up until recent years. And to top it all off, Austin was still recovering from the terror of the Servant Girl Annihilator, a serial killer of 1885. Maybe I'll write a book about him next.

Six months later, it was sold, and closed. In true Texas fashion, Colonel Driskill used all the money he made in the sale to pay off gambling debts to his brother-in-law. Since then the Driskill has had 24 separate owners. In recent years, many of those owners have been huge multinational corporations, but to their credit, they have always kept it open as "The Driskill Hotel." Everyone recognizes that this building has shaped Austin, and all of Texas, and is part of a great history.

My favorite stories are always first person accounts from people whom I have met. I have done my best to make those stories the majority of this book. The Driskill will be no exception. The room I am going to tell you about can be seen in the photo I took of the Driskill. It is the top most room on the south eastern side of the building. That room is known as the LBJ Suite.

President Lyndon Johnson had his first date with "Lady Bird" Johnson at the Driskill. They said that they fell in love in the building. Every night of the Johnson presidency, that room was rented out in the name of LBJ. This was just in case President Johnson, Lady Bird Johnson, or both were in town, they would be staying in that room. That room is the finest of the four honeymoon suites at the Driskill.

One night several years ago, I was giving a ghost tour and a couple on the tour had just gotten engaged. How do I know this? They were at the stage of love where they were telling everyone about it...nauseatingly. I am not sure how much of my stories they heard because they kept getting lost in each other's eyes. As we were leaving the Driskill that evening I heard the bride-to-be exclaim, "We should spend our wedding night here!"

I turned around and said, "Did you not hear anything that I just said?"

Apparently not, because a few months later, on their wedding night, they stayed in the LBJ Suite. As they entered the honeymoon suite, they saw that the Driskill had prepared champagne on ice and chocolate covered strawberries on a silver platter. The groom says to his bride, "Why don't you go enjoy the view from the balcony while I prepare the room?"

She obliges and goes outside to enjoy a beautiful view of 6th Street. I do not mean this in jest, from 50 feet up the lights of 6th Street can be quite charming, especially when you can escape the sound and the smell. All the balconies at the Driskill have rocking chairs on them. It's just one of the many quirks that gives this prestigious hotel a down-home feel. As the bride is looking at the sites, she notices that one of the chairs is slowly rocking. Her first thought is that she has bumped it on the way out. But it just keeps rocking.

She thought that maybe it was the wind. There wasn't enough wind to blow her dress, let alone the chair, and it just kept rocking.

About this time the groom came out with the champagne on ice and she casually mentions the rocking chair. Remember, they've taken the tour, they're OK with the idea of ghosts at the Driskill. The groom picks up the bottle of champagne and pours a glass. He holds the glass high and toasts, "To you, whomever you may be, thank you for joining us on our special night."

The rocking immediately stopped. The next day, the groom took the time out of his first day as a husband to write an email to us at the Austin Ghost Tours to tell us about their strange encounter the previous night. Stories like this are why I love the Driskill Hotel. It is a rare month that we don't get at least one new story about the Driskill, and most of them are first-hand accounts from people we have met and know, if not one of our own tour guides.

Around The Corner

"Life and death are one thread, the same line viewed from different sides."

-Laozi

If I have learned anything about the paranormal, it's that "ghosts are people, too" and their stories deserve to be told. These people are part of our history and can be a link to our past. Quite often a young person takes my tour and before we even begin they ask me if the tour is scary. They get a defeated look on their little faces when I tell them that this is a history tour, but they don't stay defeated long. My stories pull them in and suddenly they are interested in the past. My greatest triumph are the few children that have taken my tour several times through the years, became teens and even adults and they remember the stories and history year after year. I truly hope that 100 years from now I am a part of a story that someone loves to tell.

Although these are some of my favorite stories from 6th Street, this collection is barely drop in the bucket of ghost stories from around Austin. I have dozens of stories that are from buildings and businesses only blocks away from "Dirty Sixth." Putting this book together has been a true labor of love and I intend to continue my search for the supernatural in my favorite city.

I am already taking notes for my next project, "Haunted Watering Holes." In this next book we will visit bars, nightclubs, and restaurants that may not have the prestigious 6th Street address, but host paranormal guests. Until then, you can find me hosting the Austin Ghost Tours - www.AustinGhostTours.com.

ABOUT THE AUTHOR

John Maverick is a magician, storyteller, actor, alchemist, bibliophile, inventor, collector of deadly things, fire-eater, theologian, rain forest explorer, scientist, freethinker, fortuneteller, spiritualist, dreamer and snappy dresser. Maverick comes from a long line of storytellers, some professional; others reserved their gift for the dinner table. He was first introduced to the art of magic by "The Great Scott" at his fifth birthday party and Maverick has been in love with the art form ever since. Through the years he has found that he views the world around him very differently than anyone else. Maverick uses his magic to tell the story of this parallel world. Turn-Ons include: lavish hats, puns, Oxford commas, and long walks to nowhere.

Made in the USA
Monee, IL
30 October 2020

45467864R00035